MARKET CROSS, CULROSS

(Page 66)

THE
SHORES OF FIFE

Described by John Geddie
Painted by E. W. Haslehust, R.B.A.

BLACKIE AND SON LIMITED
LONDON GLASGOW AND BOMBAY

Blackie & Son's "Beautiful" Series

Beautiful England

Bath and Wells
Bournemouth and Christ-
  church
Cambridge
Canterbury
Chester and the Dee
The Cornish Riviera
Dartmoor
Dickens-Land
The Dukeries
The English Lakes
Exeter
Folkestone and Dover
Hampton Court
Hastings and Neighbourhood
Hereford and the Wye

The Isle of Wight
The New Forest
Norwich and the Broads
Oxford
The Peak District
Ripon and Harrogate
Scarborough
Shakespeare-Land
Swanage and Neighbourhood
The Thames
Warwick and Leamington
The Heart of Wessex
Winchester
Windsor Castle
York

Beautiful Scotland

Edinburgh
The Shores of Fife

Loch Lomond, Loch Katrine,
  and the Trossachs
The Scott Country

Beautiful Ireland

Connaught
Leinster

Munster
Ulster

Beautiful Switzerland

Chamonix
Lausanne and its Environs

Lucerne
Villars and Champery

LIST OF ILLUSTRATIONS

	Facing Page
Market Cross, Culross	*Frontispiece*
Forth Bridge and Coast of Fife	8
The Palace, Dunfermline	17
Aberdour	20
Cathedral Ruins, St. Andrews, from the Harbour . .	24
The Castle, St. Andrews	33
The Ruins of Lindores Abbey	37
Crail Harbour	40
Pittenweem	49
St. Monans	56
Buckhaven	60
Dysart	65

THE "KINGDOM" OF FIFE

A "Kingdom" within a kingdom — almost an
island within an island — Fife proclaims itself as a
region apart—distinct, in position and character, from
other divisions of the land. A glance at the map
suffices to show that, using the name in the older and
wider sense, Fife is set aside from its neighbours by
strongly marked frontiers. It is shaped, as the learned
George Buchanan pointed out more than three centuries
ago, like a wedge thrust out between the two Firths
that bound it, into the mists and waves of the North
Sea; and this wedge begins to be bevelled to a sharp
point at St. Andrews, where, also, its civil and ecclesiastical history starts and culminates. Across its base,
to the west, the high range of the Ochil Hills is drawn,

leaving little room between their skirts and the tidal waters of the Forth and Tay.

But little they know of Fife who know it only on paper or from without. One has to explore it, and, in particular, to go round its shore-line, to understand the success with which Nature has adapted it for the rearing of a special stock, with a history, customs, and character of their own. Neighbours all agree, and Fifers themselves have never denied, that they are a peculiar people, endowed with peculiar gifts and living in a favoured land. If, in early times, the sea and the hills cut it off from easy access to and from the surrounding provinces, Fife has always been in the swim of events, when any great crisis came in the affairs of Kirk or State; while in quieter intervals, never too extended in Scottish national annals, it gave itself to the practice of the arts of peace with a vigour and tenacity that became proverbial.

The same character, and the like fortunes, continue to cling to it. Long ago Fife discovered the secrets of making the "sundering seas" the means of traffic and the link of communication with distant countries, and of drawing forth from the bowels of the earth fuel to feed its own industries and supply the needs of other regions. More than ever does it dig power and wealth from its soil, and make use of its commanding maritime position. It produces, and uses, and ships abroad more coal, and manufactures more goods for home and foreign markets, than could have been dreamed of by the Fife men who, four centuries ago and more, began to weave linen at Dunfermline, or, at Dysart, opened pits that have since been carried far beneath the bottom of the Firth of Forth. Its colliery towns have become aggregations of human life and work, that in point of head of population at least, throw St. Andrews, to say nothing of Cupar, the sequestered little county capital in the "Howe of Fife", deep in the shade; and venerable Dunfermline has had to transform itself into a seaport by incorporating within its bounds the "Rosyth Naval Base".

The name calls to remembrance new as well as old claims by which this ancient "Kingdom by the Sea" has acquired a place of distinction and honour among the provinces of our realm and Empire. It was from the shelter of St. Margaret's Hope—the same bay of refuge where Margaret, sister of the exiled Atheling, made her landing eight and a half centuries before, to walk straight into the heart and the throne of Malcolm, and to change the whole complexion of Church and social life in Scotland—that the sea-dogs of the British navy kept watch and ward during the Great War over the safety and liberties of our islands and of the world, or, under Earl Beatty, went forth to do battle with the German High Seas Fleet off the coast of Jutland.   A son of Fife, Sir Rosslyn Erskine Wemyss, was First Lord of the British Admiralty during the final crisis of the war, while yet another, Earl Haig, of Fife descent and rearing —although actually born in Charlotte Square, Edinburgh—held chief command over the British armies in France and Flanders. Nor is it forgotten, among its titles to be taken into account in the reckoning of Imperial assets and services, that, during the greater part of the present century, the hands that held the rudder of Imperial policy were those of representatives sent to Westminster from East Fife, or from the group of burghs that included Dunfermline, Inverkeithing, and Culross.

Fife has laid strong hands on the sea ever since Sir Andrew Wood of Largo captured Stephen Bull, the English admiral, and his three ships at the back of the May Island in 1499; or six centuries earlier, when King Constantine, son of that Kenneth MacAlpin who united the kingdoms of the Picts and Scots, was slain at Fife Ness while driving the invading Danes into the salt water; back even to that more dim and uncertain date when Saint Rule, or Regulus, landed at the "Boar's Promontory", bearing with him from Achaia the bones of Andrew the Apostle, whose cross —a white saltire on a blue ground—was straightway adopted by King Hungus, the Pict, as the symbol of

FORTH BRIDGE AND COAST OF FIFE.

(Page 9)

Scotland and of victory, and whose relics gave a
new name and sanctity to the site of St. Andrews. In
these our days the bonds laid upon the subject waters
are literally forged of steel. The Forth Bridge stretches
an airy cobweb of brackets and girders, struts and stays,
across the narrows of the "Queen's Ferry"; and, on
the other side of the county, the Tay Bridge strides
across the three miles of estuary which separates Fife
from the coast of Forfar and the city of Dundee,
making of these ancient sea-passages main links
in the new, and short and easy, chain of railway
communication that binds together the South and the
North.

The Kingdom of Fife has, however, possessions in
which its inhabitants take still more pride than in its
mineral treasures, its busy seaports and factories, and
its triumphs of engineering science. There are, for
example, its rich store of ballad lore and romantic
and saintly traditions, its contributions of early or
later date to literature, art, and philosophy; its intimate
associations, all through its annals, with the great
names and great events in the history and progress
of the Scottish nation. Fife and its coasts are studded
with places that have been the homes, or temporary
residences, of Scottish royalty, and the scenes of
happenings that have had a decisive influence on
national as well as local destinies.

For, not to speak of spots like Falkland Palace and Lochleven Castle that, as being situated in the centre of the "Fifian Peninsula", lie beyond our particular field of survey, was not Dunfermline—now, as has been seen, a coast town—the favoured seat of the Scottish Court before Edinburgh? Did not Malcolm Bighead— the last King of Scotland who spoke Gaelic as his native tongue—live in the ancient tower whose fragments can still be seen in Pittencrieff Glen; and did not the saintly Margaret, his wife, say her prayers and perform her penances in the cave beside the "Crooked Linn", hard by? Are they not buried within the precincts of the great Abbey Church which their son David helped to rear in the style of Durham Cathedral, along with a host of other kings and queens, including Robert the Bruce, and James III and James V of Scots, one of whom began, while the other completed, the Palace which adjoins and partly occupies the site of the renowned Benedictine Monastery? Were not some of these and other members of the line of Banquo—with happy, or much more often unhappy, fortunes awaiting them—born in this royal dwelling under the shadow of the Abbey Barbican, and among them Charles I, the "Martyr King", of whom, while still in his cradle, his sapient father said he was "a girnin' bairn" over whom "the Deil has cussin his cloak"?

Or, to extend the field of vision to places of lesser

standing, although, to the Fife eye at least, by no means undeserving of note, did not James VI and I do honour to that most antiquated of old Scottish burghs, Culross—also the seat of an abbey and the birthplace of Glasgow's patron saint, Mungo—by lodging in the ramshackle edifice still known as the "Palace", while inspecting the first coal-mining experiments under the sea-bottom carried out by his host, Sir George Bruce of Carnock? Had not Mary, Queen of Scots, associations with Rosyth Castle, the grey keep that now stands sentinel over the docks and derricks of the Naval Base? Had not Annabella Drummond, the consort of Robert III, and mother of the royal author of the *King's Quhair*, her palace in Inverkeithing, of which some walls and vaults remain? Did not Queen Yolande, the bride of Alexander III, wait for the coming of her husband to the castle on Kinghorn Ness on that fateful night—"the worst that Scotland had ever known"— when he was flung from his horse while riding home- ward from the Ferry along the shore rocks? Was it not at Rossend Castle that the poet Chastelard com- mitted the culminating folly of hiding in the bed-chamber of Mary Stewart, that brought him to the block; and in the Kirk of Burntisland close by that Mary's son announced the design that bore fruit in the Authorized Version of the Bible? It was at Wemyss Castle, farther east, that Mary first saw and was taken by the goodly outer person of the "lang lad" Darnley; and at the East Neuk, beyond Crail, that Mary's mother stepped ashore on the Scottish soil where she was to meet a larger portion of sorrow than of happiness.

Many, also, are the filaments in the warp and woof of the story of the royal line that are attached to Balmerino and Lindores Abbeys, to Ballenbriech and Ferry-Port-on-Craig, and other spots on the northern fringes of Fife. But towards St. Andrews all the threads in the history of the Scottish monarchy, and of the Scottish Kirk and State, seem to converge, and to be wrought into a pattern of strong and sombre colouring. It may seem strange that the Primacy of the Church, and the earliest home of academic learning in an ancient realm, should be set in a corner so remote and difficult of access—the peninsula of a peninsula, which in our more frivolous days has become a place of holiday resort, known chiefly as the "Mecca of Golf". But the "Grey City by the Sea" must in all ages have exercised a resistless pull on the hearts and fancies of many diverse kinds of pilgrims—lovers of nature and fresh air and lovers of learning; "gowfers" and antiquaries.

Numerous are the ties that connect the fortunes of St. Andrews with those of the Scottish Crown. Robert the Bruce went there to be anointed king, and to be present at the consecration, in 1318, by his great friend

and supporter, Bishop Lamberton, of the Cathedral
which had been founded 160 years before by Malcolm
the Maiden.   Mary of Lorraine entered the town in
State, and, coming fresh from the Court of France,
declared that not even there had she seen "so many
good faces in so little room".   Mary, her daughter,
spent a pleasant time as a "burgess's wife", in the old
town, in a house which has not yet been wiped out of
existence.   Much less agreeable were the experiences
of Charles II, who visited St. Andrews during the reign
of the "Saints of the Covenant" after the crowning at
Scone and before Worcester fight, and was soundly
lectured on doctrine by Samuel Rutherford and rated
on conduct by Robert Blair.

More even than the history of the monarchy has the
history of the Scottish Church revolved around Fife.
St. Andrews has been its ecclesiastical centre almost
from the date when St. Rule, escaping from shipwreck,
took refuge in the cave not far from the antique tower
that bears his name.   It was, however, the Church
Council held here in 1074, whereat the country was first
divided into dioceses, and the appointment to the see
of Turgot, Queen Margaret's confessor and biographer,
that conferred on it definite prominence and precedence.
Then, also, began in earnest the Church reform struggle
that ended in the expulsion of the Culdees, who from
time immemorial had had their foundation on the Kirk

Heugh, and whose arts and influence are perhaps best attested by the extraordinary wealth of sculptured Celtic monuments which have been found in and around the Cathedral. It was the beginning, too, of the much longer conflict for the imposition on Scotland of the ecclesiastical jurisdiction of England, which, starting with the consecration of Turgot by the York Chapter, took many forms threatening the independence of the country, before it was finally closed by the erection of St. Andrews into an archbishopric in 1474.

The Bishops and the Archbishops of St. Andrews were well in the front of all the civil and religious broils of the "Kingdom" in the centuries before, and in the generations immediately following, the Reformation; and also, it is only fair to say, in good works, for the advancement of knowledge, and for the beautifying of the place of their habitation. While helping forward the Cathedral work, they found time and means for the rearing of priories, chantries, and episcopal palaces. In 1200 Bishop Roger began building the castle; a couple of generations later Bishop Wishart founded the Blackfriars Monastery; the patriot Bishop Lamberton helped mightily to turn the tide that rose to victory at Bannockburn; Bishop Bennet, who was taken prisoner at Neville's Cross with David Bruce, lived to crown the first of the Stewart kings; Bishop Wardlaw, if he burned Lollardist heretics, built the Guard Bridge

over the Eden, and founded the University; Bishop
Kennedy was the munificent founder and endower of
St. Salvator's College, where his monument is one of
the triumphs of the renascence art of his day; and
Bishop Alexander Stewart, to whom St. Andrews owes
St. Leonard's College, died by his father's side on
Flodden Field.

Then following on the brief and stormy archi-
episcopate of Gawain Douglas, the translator of Virgil,
we come to those tragic chapters in the chronicles of
Fife and of Scotland inscribed with the names of the
Beatons, James and David, uncle and nephew, Archbishop and Cardinal. The chief acts in the drama, in
which John Knox also had a leading part, were played
in St. Andrews. James was that rapacious and domi-
neering churchman who, when he appeared, with his
priest's robe over his armour, in the Edinburgh street-
scrimmage known as "Cleanse the Causey", beat his
breast while vowing that his conscience was free of the
knowledge that there was any strife afoot, and received
the stinging retort: "Your conscience clatters, my
Lord!" He set the heather on fire by burning in front
of his episcopal residence the first martyr of the
Scottish Reformation, Patrick Hamilton, of whom it
is said that "his reek infected all on whom it blew".
Yet it was James Beaton who founded St. Mary's
College, completed by his successor, Archbishop Ham-

ilton, and he is said to have made a godly end in exile in France. In pride and ambition, as well as in luxury, the nephew—the Scottish Wolsey—surpassed the uncle. Cardinal Beaton has left an ugly mark in the civil and religious annals of a period of violent change, although perhaps more can be said for the man and the churchman than the zealots of his age would allow. He sealed his fate when, following the evil example of his relative and predecessor, he burned George Wishart at the stake, he himself, according to the story, looking down on the scene from a seat above the castle gateway.

Vengeance did not tarry long. It came in the form of Norman Lesley and his fellow conspirators, who, in 1546, when the drawbridge was down to admit new building material for Beaton's "Babylon", broke into the castle and savagely murdered the Cardinal. Sir David Lyndesay, the chief poet of Fife and of Scotland in the era, wrote the epitaph on the man and his end:

"Although the loon was well away
The deed was foully done".

Knox was among the besieged Reformers in the castle, and he left it as a prisoner condemned to labour in the French galleys. But he returned later, when the gale of the Reformation was at its height, to "ride in the whirlwind and direct the storm" on the heads of his enemies, the opposers of the new doctrines.

THE PALACE, DUNFERMLINE

(Page 10)

Nowhere did the tempest rage more furiously than in St. Andrews and the East Neuk of Fife. It tore the roof from the Cathedral, and scattered its ornaments and endowments to the four winds. There are left only bare walls and pinnacles that seem to fling up gaunt arms on the breezy headland, appealing against their fate and against those who wrought their destruction. The Town Kirk, in which Knox, and afterwards that "Presbyterian Boanerges" Andrew Melville, "dang the pulpit to blauds" in denouncing the wickednesses of their time, took the place of the Great Church of St. Andrew as the centre of inspiration of the Church polity of Scotland. Knox himself led forth the multitude who set about cleansing the land of the "monuments of idolatary", beginning with those of the neighbouring "weel-aired toon of Crail".

The new creed and the new form of Church government were not to bring peace, but a sword, to these uttermost parts of the shores of Fife and to the rest of Scotland, as the following century and a quarter, during which Presbytery and Episcopacy were alternately in the ascendant, was to prove. Incidents of that long and intricate religious and secular struggle were the hanging of Archbishop Hamilton at Stirling, and the murder of Archbishop Sharp on Magus Muir. Fife flung herself with vehement energy into the "Wars of the Covenant", and the blood of her sons was poured out like water on the fields of Tibbermuir and Kilsyth, where the "Great Montrose"—himself at one time a student at St. Andrews and a Covenanter—broke and slaughtered their ranks.   It bred a particularly dour and fiery species of zealot, of the type of Balfour of Burley and Hackston of Rathillet, principals in the unpremeditated crime that made an end of "Sharp of that Ilk", who also, from a supporter, had become the relentless enemy of the Presbyterian cause.   In the end the "blue blanket" triumphed.   But without venturing into the deep and drumly waters of ecclesiastical controversy, it may be noted that Secession and Dissent in the eighteenth century had their origin, and some of their most remarkable developments, in Fife; and that Dr. Thomas Chalmers, the leader of the "Disruption", was a son of Anstruther, minister of Kilmany, and a professor in St. Andrews, where also have flourished, and flourish to this hour, choice and characteristic examples of the fervour and eloquence, the humour and the learning, the diversities of opinion and belief, and the underlying and, it may be hoped, now growing and prevailing spirit of unity within the Christian Church—using that word in its wider sense —planted ages ago in this secluded corner, and since watered, or scalded, so plenteously with blood and tears.

This glance over the troubled background of St. Andrews' history, so full of storm and stress, of shafts of sunlight and wisps of "haar", seems necessary for those who would rightly appreciate the aspect and atmosphere of the old university town, which lives so much in its past. Besides, not only is it the fount and origin, the "abstract and brief epitome", of the annals of Fife, as Fife is of the story of Scotland. Its architectural and topographical features are found repeated, on a reduced scale and with less emphasis, all around the coast line which King Jamie compared to a "fringe of gold on a beggar's mantle". St. Andrews is the microcosm of a microcosm. The cells and caves, and wells of saints and hermits, heroes and martyrs, are dotted along the shores of Fife in situations of which those of St. Rule's and Kinkell furnish the type—St. Adrian's at Caiplie and Pittenweem; St. Monan's at Kilminning and St. Monans; St. Serf's at Dysart; the "Black Cave" of Constantine at Fife Ness; Macduff's Caves at Kincraig and Wemyss, among the rest. Crombie, Rosyth, and Dalgety; Burntisland and Kinghorn, the Chapel Towers at West Wemyss and the Chapel Ness of Earlsferry; Balmerino and Flisk; these make but an incomplete list of the ancient churchyards and church fabrics—mostly roofless and deserted—that, like St. Andrews Cathedral and its mouldering stones, lean over the sea margin and listen to the dirge of the waves breaking on skerry and beach.

Still more thickly studded along the shore-line, and often taking, like the Bishop's Palace of St. Andrews, the sea and the cliffs for main defence, are the castles of the Fife coast. Some of them, such as Wemyss and Rossend, are yet inhabited, and have chambers that harbour ghosts and traditions that carry us far back into the mists of the past. Others, as for example Aberdour, Donibristle, Seafield, Pathhead, Ravenscraig, Ardross, Newark, and Ballenbriech, are roofless shells, the shadows of their former strength and importance; and to this category belonged, until recent years, Rosyth Castle, whose walls have been patched up to serve as a club for the officers stationed at the Naval Base. Still others have their sites indicated only by a few broken walls or grassy mounds, or by a name; and of these are Dunimarle and Duniquarle, Kingsbarns and Kinkell. Generally the Fife keep or manor house, whether on the sea or inland, has its pigeon-house in close attendance—it was the inseparable appurtenance of a "Fife lairdship", together, according to the local proverb, with a "wee pickle land, a big pickle debt, and a lawsuit". Sometimes the "doo-cot", a picturesque feature set on foreland or recess, is seen to have abided the assaults of time and weather more sturdily than its more dignified

ABERDOUR

(Page 22)

companion; it has been thriftily repaired, while the other has been left to go to decay.

The islands, too, that lie off the shores of Fife, have their legends and relics of saintly and feudal times that might easily fill a volume—Preston Island, with its memories of the smuggling days; Inchgarvie, with its castle, blotted out by the Forth Bridge works, that has been a State prison; Inchkeith, now become a fortified guardian and beacon of the fairway of the Firth; Mugdrum with its cross. More noteworthy than these, reminders of an age when sanctity was intimately associated with isolation from the haunts of men, are Inchcolm and the May, each of them the seat of a religious house, the seed of which was first planted in the midst of these stormy waters by some solitude-seeking anchorite, to be afterwards raised to be a priory, and endowed with lands and gifts by the piety of kings and nobles. The chapter house and refectory of the Augustinian Priory of Inchcolm, founded in 1123 by Alexander the Fierce in gratitude for being saved from shipwreck, remain, and the tower continues to be a far-seen object by those who sail the waters or pace the shores of Fife. It looks across "Mortimer's Deep"—into which, says legend, the monks of that "nocht obscure monastar" dropped the body of one of their benefactors, whose bequest they prized more than his person—to the beautiful sweep of Aberdour

Bay and the castle of the Douglases, Earls of Morton. Hard by Aberdour lie the woods of Donibristle, the heritage of the "Bonnie Earl of Moray", who was slain by the Gordons on the shore below the ruined house which preserves, in an unburned wing, some relics of the deed.

If "Saint Colm's Inch", in which "Sweno, Norway's king", paid ransom for the privilege of burying his dead after his defeat by Macbeth, be dedicated to the fiery, island-loving Irish missionary to the heathen Picts, the May Island cherishes the memory of the martyred Adrian and of Monan, slain by the Northmen. They were two of the many obscure saints who, if not indigenous to Fife, were greatly revered within its bounds. Its monks, also, of the Order of Canons Regular, found firmer and wider footing at Pittenweem, on the adjoining mainland. But the island, the site of the first beacon in these waters, and still, like Inchkeith, a guiding light to navigators of the Firth of Forth, long continued to be a place of pilgrimage and penance for the faithful and the credulous.

Fife, as will be seen, and especially its shore-line, has a savour of its own; and, as has been written, it is best discovered and appreciated under grey skies and in breezy weather, in the winter or early spring, when most of the tourists and summer residents have deserted the beach, and the "gowfers" are few on the links. "Only after you have faced the wind from the North Sea that plies its untiring rasp on the edge of the headlands, and shrills round the seaward projections and callosities of the ancient buildings down by the shore, can you trust yourself to read aright the quaint hieroglyphic of Nature's handiwork and man's, that is written along the margin of the Fife coast. The little burghs huddling under the shelter of cape and high ground; the red-tiled, steep-ridged houses crowding together and turning their crow-stepped gables and forestairs to the street and their backs to the blast; the forlorn little graveyards on the brink of the salt water, each with its group of old tombstones and storm-stressed trees, gathered about some fragment of ivied ruin; the Dutch-looking kirk-spire and town-house steeple, sturdily asserting themselves beside the new school-house and literary institute; holy caves and wells under a canopy of pit-smoke; dilapidated salt-pan, and malt-barn, and doo-cot, standing cheek-by-jowl with present-day villa and factory-stalk—all are seen to be native to the element and the scene. They have that indurated, strongly-marked individuality which belongs to Fife character as well as to Fife architecture. They are the expression of all the past weather and past history of the province."

As we have partly seen, another thread besides that of the royal line of Malcolm and of Banquo is stitched

into the hem of Fife—that which records the story and
marks the trail of the line of Macduff. History tells us
nothing of a "Thane of Fife". The hero, "not of
woman born", who slew the tyrant Macbeth, was
probably descended from the Celtic kings of the
province; and the privileges enjoyed by him and his
successors may have been the reward of services and
sacrifices, going back into the dim ages behind the
reign of Canmore, the memory of which is now only
vaguely preserved in legend, custom, and folklore.
They included the right of placing the king on the
"Stone of Destiny" at Scone, of leading his forces in
battle, and, still more prized, perhaps, in a lawless
age, of obtaining remission for "sudden chaudmelle", or
unpremeditated slaughter, by the offer of compensation
to the next of kin, on a regulated scale, within the
sanctuary of "Cross Macduff" by the homicide who
was related, within the ninth degree, to the chief of
the clan. The pedestal of the cross, mentioned in
a charter by Canmore to Macduff, holds its place in a
pass through the Ochils, behind Newburgh, "commanding" as Sir Walter Scott writes:

> "Prospect wide o'er field and fell,
> And peopled village and extended moorland,
> And the wide ocean and majestic Tay,
> To the far-distant Grampians".

It originally bore an inscription, now obliterated, that
has "foiled philologists", but the purport of which

CATHEDRAL RUINS, ST. ANDREWS, FROM THE HARBOUR

(Page 31)

was understood to be obeyed by the refugee, when he grasped one of the nine rings let into the rude stone, washed nine times in the "Nine Wells" spring, and paid "nine cows and a colpendach", or young cow, to the avenger of blood.

The "privilege of Clan Macduff" continued to be claimed down to the close of the sixteenth century. The right of leading the van of the royal army was lost earlier. The title of Hereditary Standard Bearer, possessed by the family of the Scrymgeour-Wedderburns of Birkhill, a few miles east of Newburgh, commemorates a later patriotic service rendered in Wallace's time by Scrymgeour, the valiant Constable of Dundee. The prerogative of setting the king on the throne was exercised by generation after generation of the Earls of Fife; it may be remembered that Isabel, Countess of Fife, for performing this hereditary duty at the crowning of the Bruce, was confined in a cage hung outside the walls of Dunbar Castle. The last time the honour fell to the old line was when Duncan, Earl of Fife, crowned James I of Scots, at Scone; a year later, their lands and titles, including Falkland, were declared forfeited and appropriated by the Stewarts. Falkland may have been their head-quarters, but the race of Macduff had many strongholds and wide lands on the Fife coast.

Macbeth, who ruled wisely and firmly for seventeen

years and was the first Scottish king to visit Rome and receive a blessing at the hands of the Pope, has also set his hand and seal on it. He won his victory at Bordie, between Culross and Kincardine-on-Forth, and, with his wife, was a benefactor of the Culdees of Lochleven and St. Andrews.

Macduff, and the Macduff legend, are symbols of the Celtic element, obscurely but pervasively blended in the history, the customs, and the character of the "Folk of Fife". It manifests itself strongly in the place-names of the region, which are distinctively and predominantly Celtic; nowhere else, outside or inside the Highlands, do "Bals" and "Pits"—the equivalent of the Anglo-Saxon "ton" or "ham"—more abound. It declares itself in the traits and ways of the inhabitants, whether dwellers on the coast or inland; "to be a Fifer is next-door to being a Hielandman", says the proverb. And yet in pawkiness and in prudence, as in courage in war, enterprise in peace, and pride of race, they are Scots of the Scots; and nowhere, in poetry or in prose, has the "braid Scots tongue" been wielded with more pith and pungency. Gaelic—or was it Pictish?—has ceased to be spoken in Fife for many centuries; it was among the first districts to shed the clan system and to adopt feudalism. Yet there continue to linger words and phrases, ideas and habits, that seem to claim descent from the age when Malcolm spoke in a Celtic tongue to the neighbours who gathered around him at Pittencrieff, or at Markinch; and Fifers are Lowland Scots "with a difference".

This indigenous strain, along with many alien influences—from Holland, Scandinavia and France, as well as from across the Firths and across the Border—is revealed even in the church and domestic architecture of the "Kingdom"; but most of all, perhaps, in its literature. Some of the choicest flowers of ballad and lyric poetry have rooted and blossomed along the coast of Fife; and all of them have a "tang of the soil". "Sir Patrick Spens" strode on the sands of Aberdour, and the "Bonnie Earl o' Moray" was slaughtered at Donibristle. "Auld Robin Gray", "The Boatie Rows", "Maggie Lauder", and the original version of "Auld Lang Syne" sprang up on or near the Fifian shore. The Fife witches, the Fife lairds, the Fife matrons and maidens—

> "The saucy kimmers o' Largo,
>   And the bonnie lasses o' Leven"—

have been celebrated in strains that are held in perpetual remembrance, at least in their place of birth. The "Gude and Godlie Ballates", came from a Dunfermline schoolmaster of the sixteenth century; the "Ode to the Cuckoo" from a dominie of Kinnesswood; "Hardiknute", an imitation of the ancient ballad that deceived many literary experts, was the production of

Lady Wardlaw of Pitreavie, behind Inverkeithing, who is suspected of being the maker, or shaper, of other pieces that have been admitted into the canon of the antique. Sir David Lyndesay of the Mount—of the same name and race as the authoress of "Auld Robin Gray" —was like other poets of the pre- and post-Reformation periods, a Fife landowner, and his "Ane Pleasant Satyre of the Thrie Estaitis" was played on the Castle-hill of Cupar.

Fife literary genius has been wont to express itself in biting satire, or, like Fife art in the canvases of Sir David Wilkie, in broadly humorous and racily natural studies of human life and character, such as are to be found in old ditties like "The Wife of Auchtermuchty" and "The Wee Cooper of Fife", or, in more elaborate form, in the "flyting", or "midden polemic", between the villagers of neighbouring townships, contained in the Latin macaronics of William Drummond, and in the "Anster Fair" of Professor Tennant. More plainly almost than in verse, these combined qualities of strong realism and vivid imagination have been reflected in the prose literature to which Fife has given birth. Lindsay of Pitscottie's "History" and the "Diary" of James Melville, minister of Easter Anstruther, are rightfully regarded as classics of Middle and Early Jacobean Scots—when Scots was still a Court language and Fife a region where it was spoken in its purest and pithiest.

Before and since Scott, many novelists, essayists, and rhymsters have come to its shores for fresh inspiration. St. Andrews itself, in intervals when the hands and thoughts of "the City of the Scarlet Gown" were not absorbed in theology, science, and philosophy, or in golf, has been a nest of singing birds, and has had Robert Ferguson and John Campbell Shairp among its students or professors.

ST. ANDREWS

Thus all the trails in the art and literature, and in the legendary and authentic history of the region, lead us back to St. Andrews, just as all the roads that wind around the coasts or climb across the hills of Eastern Fife seem to find their way to "the Pends". In the ancient city itself the three broad thoroughfares of South Street, Market Street, and North Street converge, like the ribs of a fan, in the direction of the Cathedral ruins—to draw our feet and thoughts back into the past. By whichever of its main avenues the traveller by rail directs his steps eastward through the town he finds the vista closed by the monuments of its departed greatness; just as he who approaches it by road, from the side of Crail and the East Neuk, or across the inland hills from Anstruther, Largo, or Cupar, sees from afar the tall Tower of St. Rule, and a gaunt eastern gable and a twisted pinnacle of the west front of the ruined Metropolitan Church, graven against a background of sea and sky, as symbols of what the city has been.

Each of the three broad and wind-swept streets might be taken as representing a phase of St. Andrews annals, or a leading element in its growth and destiny. In the spacious, lime-fringed South Street, still entered through the gateway in the old walls, called the West Port, we are treading the Way of the Church. It leads straight to the entrance to the Cathedral and Priory. The tower and spire and restored fabric of the Trinity or Town Church—the building from which Knox and Melville thundered against Popery and Prelacy—flank it on the left; on the other side of the way is a beautiful fragment of the Blackfriars Monastery, in front of Madras College; farther on is St. Mary's College—on the site of the "Pedagogium", the earliest of the St. Andrews educational foundations—which gives housing to the theological faculty and to the library of the modern University; while nearer the shadow of the Cathedral walls are the roofless remains of the Chapel and College of St. Leonard's, the hospice turned by the liberality of Prior Hepburn into a school of learning, which, perhaps, did more to spread abroad the tenets of the Reformation, and to lay the Ancient Church in ruins, than any other building in the land. Market Street is the traditional centre of the mercantile movement and of the municipal authority of St. Andrews, although the Town Hall and Cross have been removed from its fairway to other sites; while North Street is even more distinctively than South Street the head-quarters of the academical activities of the place,

since it contains the United College of St. Salvator
and St. Leonard and the venerable College Chapel,
in which are enshrined the choicest of the memories
and relics of this earliest of Scottish Universities.

Time was, according to legend, when St. Andrews
had a fourth spoke in her radiating quadrant of streets,
represented by the "Swallowgate", now known as "The
Scores". It stood, in earlier, and it stands still more
emphatically in these later times, where only a broken
line of houses faces the links and the sea, for the
strenuous sport that has always mingled with the more
serious thoughts and labours of St. Andrews. For if
its neighbours to the south speak eloquently of the
piety, the trade, and the learning of the past and the
present, "The Scores" talks of golf, and of little else;
unless, in the vicinity of the castle and the Martyrs'
Monument, of the "Witch Hill" and the "Smugglers'
Cave", discourse turns to "old unhappy far-off things",
or to sea-bathing.

"Gowf", indeed, has done more to rehabilitate St.
Andrews than parliamentary grants and Royal Com-
missions. The fame of the "Royal and Ancient" Club
is blown more widely about the globe than that of the
Cathedral and University; and the hazards of the
Swilcan Burn and the "Cardinal's Nose" have been the
occasion of more debate than the fate of George
Wishart, David Beaton, or James Sharp. Among the

THE CASTLE, ST. ANDREWS

(Page 35)

visitors to this part of the coast of Fife, familiar with every bunker and green on the course, are many who neither know nor care whether Prior Hepburn was the founder of St. Mary's College, and Bishop Kennedy—the occupant of the magnificent tomb in the College Chapel— was the institutor of St. Salvator's, or *vice versa*. They neither know, nor care to know, that George Buchanan, the great Latinist, was Principal of St. Leonard's; that Calderwood and Rutherford, Chalmers and Tulloch, Gregory and Brewster taught in St. Andrews class-rooms. Their interest in the "Great Montrose" is not that he was the "Skaith of Fife", but that he played on the Links, and won the silver arrow at the Bow Butts; and they take note of the Cathedral ruins chiefly because "Old Tom" and "Young Tommie" Morris are buried under their shadow, or because their towers, rather than the steeple of the Town Kirk, make a convenient mark in driving the ball towards the Home Hole.

The Royal Game is the elixir that, within the past century, has resuscitated St. Andrews, brought, through religious wars and revolutions, and subsequent neglect, to low estate. All through the seventeenth and eighteenth centuries its fortunes were at ebb; and perhaps low-water mark was reached when, in 1697, it was proposed to remove the University to Perth, because St. Andrews had become "only a village, where

for the most part farmers dwell; the whole streets are
filled with dunghills, which are exceeding noisome and
infect the air, especially in the season when the herring-
guts are exposed in them ". But at a much later date
its condition and prospects continued to be parlous.
The town was bankrupt; a sixth or more of the dwellings were in ruins, and the "middens" remained a burning question. The professors were starving, and the
class-rooms empty. St. Andrews, within its cincture of
crumbling walls and under its toppling monuments of
antiquity, looked like a withered nut in its husk. Dr.
Samuel Johnson, who came here in 1773, and behaved
in a more than ordinarily bearish manner to the
University magnates who sought to do him honour,
spoke of it as a blend of squalor and magnificence; but
the magnificence was of the past.

Then came the magic touch of golf, and, aided by an
enterprising Provost of Early Victorian date, Sir Hugh
Playfair, the place began to revive and burgeon — to
build up its waste places and to extend its Elysian
Fields, until now they stretch almost to Out Head and
the mouth of the Eden estuary. The University as
well as the town has benefited; and the Scarlet Gown
helps to give vivid touches of colour to the streets,
as does the Red Coat to the Links, where representatives of the Navy and the Army, of Law, Medicine, and
Divinity, of Commerce and of Labour, disport them-

selves, while the praises of their healthful and inspiring air have been sung by poets and historians, novelists and essayists, like Andrew Lang and Mrs. Oliphant and Anthony Trollope, Longfellow and "A. K. H. B.".

Even the most absorbed of golfers might spare a thought for the Castle—the "Castle by the sea", around which "the winds and the waves of ocean" keep buffeting, long after the storms of war, that beat around it for many centuries, have sunk to rest. The building is now only an empty shell. Below the moat and Fore Tower, whose function as gateway to the Castle has lately been established, run subterranean passages which extend under the streets of the burgh. In the centre of the grass-grown courtyard is the Castle well. In one seaward corner stands the Sea Tower, and below it that grim reminder of the tender mercies of mediæval times, the "Bottle Dungeon". It was "in a nuke at the bottom of the Sea Tower", according to Knox's statement, that "God's children" were kept, while awaiting their fate; and in it the body of the Cardinal himself was "pickled in brine" and was concealed before sepulture. The prevailing atmosphere is tragic, as is that surrounding the once magnificent Cathedral and the adjoining Abbey—more accurately Priory—entry to which was made through the spacious archways of the Pends.

The Abbey walls are in good condition, and retain

many of their defences and embellishments of gate-
ways, towers, and niches.   The foundations of the
Priory have been excavated, and the walls and arches
partly rebuilt, and, with the extant remains of the
Guest House, Tithe Barn, and Abbey Mill, reveal something of the former state of this mother-house of the
other Augustinian monasteries in Fife, once renowned
for its wealth and splendour.   The Cathedral itself,
the labour and the joy of many generations, has been
a melancholy wreck ever since the day of

> "Steir, stramash and strife,
> Whan bickerin' frae the touns o' Fife,
> Great bands o' bodies, thick and rife,
>   Gaed to Sanct Androis toun,
> And wi' John Calvin i' their heads,
> And hammers i' their hands and spades,
> Enraged at idols, mass and beads,
>   Dang the Cathedral doon".

Neglect, greed, and vandalism completed the destruction begun by Knox's "rascal multitude".   The great
cruciform church, 358 feet long, and 160 feet across
the transepts—indications have recently been found
that the nave was once longer by several bays—was
begun about 1160, and completed, under the eye of
eleven successive bishops, a century and a half later.
There now remain only parts of the western front,
eastern gable, southern wall of the nave, and western
side of the south transept and chapter house, together
with some broken pillars, maimed arches, round and

THE RUINS OF LINDORES ABBEY

(Page 41)

pointed, and shattered window tracery. All is open to
the sky, and in places the Metropolitan Church, which
has witnessed some of the chief scenes of Scottish
history, has been pillaged and overthrown, down to
the very foundations.

In contrast, there stands up, close by and yet apart,
the Romanesque Tower of St. Regulus, probably or
possibly the predecessor of the twelfth century fabric,
and destined, in its four-square massive strength, long to
outlast it even in ruin; while still a little farther to the
east, between the Abbey wall and the sea, we reach a
yet lower stratum of ecclesiastical art and history in the
fragment of the Culdee foundation of St. Mary-at-the-
Kirkheugh. Here we are close to the eastern boundary of St. Andrews, and overlook the little harbour—
originally a creek at the mouth of the Kinness burn—
and the sandy and rocky shores that stretch towards
Buddo Ness and the East Neuk.

Dr. Johnson thought St. Andrews "eminently
adapted for study". This is true in even a larger
sense than was meant by the Great Whale of literature.
The quest of nature and of history, like the pursuit
of the "jeuking ba'", can be engaged in with singular
zest and with peculiar reward in this delectable corner
of the "Kingdom". The sea as well as the land opens
its treasures. It is the seat of a marine laboratory;
the botanist finds a happy hunting-ground by the

Lade Braes or round the old house of Kinkell, or farther afield on Magus or Tents Muir, or in Dura Den. Sir Archibald Geikie has said that if he were asked to name a place in the three Kingdoms—almost in Europe—"where geology could be best taught practically by an appeal directly to Nature", he would unhesitatingly name St. Andrews. But as much might almost be said of any spot selected for residence and exploration in the East Neuk. It is "the classic region for the study of volcanoes and volcanic action". In pre-organic and prehistoric, as in historical times, there was always something lively doing on the Shores of Fife.

NORTHWARDS
FROM ST. ANDREWS

It is true that, to the north of the town, beyond the estuary of the Eden, and on towards the entrance to the Firth of Tay, lies a waste and barren land, with few outstanding features and scant history— Tents Muir. But even this territory of windlestrae and sand-hills, flat foreshore and marshy pastures, is interesting as the resort of many varieties of wild fowl, and temporary place of exile of Pallas's sand-grouse, and also as formerly the abode of a race of smugglers and wreckers, who were said to be the descendants of the survivors of a Danish fleet wrecked on Abertay Sands. To reach it one has to go round by Guard Bridge, where close at hand are the Castlehill and the Kirk of Leuchars, with its double-arcaded apse —a gem of Norman architecture—and its memories of Alexander Henderson and the Covenant, and the well-preserved sixteenth-century mansion of Earlshall on the site of a castle of the Macduffs.

At the extremity of these heathery and sandy tracts we look across the Tay to Barry Links, and out to sea, where the Bell Rock is the only scrap of land between us and Jutland. Farther west, Ferry-Port-on-Craig, or Tayport, opposes Broughty Castle on the northern shore. Here, under the Craig, was the first and at one time the most famous of sea-water ferries. It has seen, and still sees, many adventurous passages between Angus and Fife. But the Tay Bridge, which, beyond Newport, strides across the Firth in many spans to where the shipping and buildings of Dundee are piled along the front and around the bases of The Law and Balgay Hill, has stripped it of its importance, which has, in part, passed over to its neighbour Newport. Scotscraig is behind it, a possession of Archbishop Sharpe, and, long before his time, of Michael Scott, from whom it may take its name. No wizardry of that ancient date, in "bridling the flood with a curb of stone", can compare with the feat of the modern engineer in flinging a structure of steel from bank to bank across more than two miles of sea-water. Yet there was one wild night, in December, 1879, when the wind and the waves had their triumph, and the centre of the structure plunged into the sea with a passenger train and all that it carried.

Above Wormit and the Tay Bridge, the Firth widens, and the northern shore of Fife looks across to the rich lands of the Carse of Gowrie, a country of fertile fields and spreading woods and old castles and mansions, backed by the Sidlaw Hills, and behind

CRAIL HARBOUR

(Page 46)

these, and away to the west, the distant peaks of the
Grampians. The Fife hills draw nearer the coast,
and in Norman's Law and other heights show a bold
front—the beginning of the Ochils; and hamlets and
historic manor houses, old battlefields, churches and
castles, and a couple of venerable abbeys are inserted
between their steep green or forest-clad slopes and
the "Broad Water".

Of the Castle of Naughton, the home of a legendary
chieftain of the Hay family, whom Gawain Douglas, in
his "Palace of Honour", placed alongside Robin Hood
and other heroes of romance, only a few ruins are left.
But the grey walls of Ballanbreich, or Bambreich, stand
out boldly on a steep bank overhanging the shore,
a landmark of the upper Firth.

The abbeys are Balmerino and Lindores. Of the
former, founded by Queen Ermengarde, the wife of
William the Lion and mother of Alexander II, and
dedicated to the Virgin and St. Edward the Confessor,
all that remain are some arcaded arches and vaulted
apartments. There is nothing to mark the tomb of
the founder before the high altar. The monks fell into
bad repute before the Reformation, and the buildings
went to utter decay. The lands were given to the
Elphinstone family, and the latest holders of the title
of Lord Balmerino won a melancholy fame for their
devotion to the House of Stewart.

Lindores Abbey has a greater record behind it, and has more to show above ground. It stood near the road from the Howe of Fife, where it comes down, past Lindores Loch and the ruins of Magidrin's church and through the little glen that skirts the relics of Denmyln Castle—the home of a family of Balfours, one of whom, Sir James, the antiquary, was of the ten Lord Lyons drawn from Fife in a century — to meet the coast road on the eastern margin of the little royal burgh of Newburgh. It is ground haunted by the traditional and the real figures of Scotland's past. The foundations of yet another "Macduff's Castle" are hard by the forked ways; as has been seen, "Macduff's Cross" is hidden in the hills behind. The Sculptured Cross of Mugdrum is on the march between Fife and Perth, and ahead, the Round Tower and the poplars of Abernethy, the ancient Pictish capital, show up like the boundary marks of another province of national history. Wallace's Camp, before his victory of Blackearnside, is a little way behind us; Edward Longshanks, John Balliol, David Bruce and other royal personages sojourned in the Tyronesian Abbey, which was founded in the twelfth century by David, Earl of Huntingdon, heir to the throne and hero of the "Talisman", and dedicated by him to St. Mary and St. Andrew, in gratitude for having taken the city of Ptolomais, and for having been saved from shipwreck. The body of his unfortunate descendant and namesake, David, Duke of Rothesay, was buried here in a stone coffin, now empty, and it wrought miracles until his brother, James I of Scots, began to wreak vengeance on his murderers, when, as Hector Boece says, they "ceassit finally". Here too, a couple of generations later, came James, ninth Earl of Douglas —"Greystiel"—to join, after a stormy life, the company of the religious, and to console himself with his stoic philosophy—"He that can do no better must be a monk".

The groined arch of the entrance to the cloisters is the chief feature left of the once extensive and wealthy monastery, whose lands were acquired by, and gave a title to, the Leslies. The orchard trees in which the neighbourhood is embowered may be another gift of the monks, who are said to have first planted pear trees in the district. The main street of Newburgh changes but slowly with the passage of time; nor is there usually much bustle down by the Shore, where the Firth contracts to the dimensions of a tidal stream before reaching the meeting of the valleys of the Tay and Earn, overhung by the green Ochils and the rocks and woods of Moncrieffe and Kinnoul Hills. The hand-loom-weaving of the place is long extinct, but it has other business that keeps it alive; it retains along with its proverbial spirit of independence the affection of visitors who know the road to this secluded recess in the unfrequented section of the Shores of Fife over which we have cast a hasty glance.

ROUND THE EAST NEUK

For the full salt savour of Fife, we must move from these brackish waters and more sheltered shores to another corner of the land—to the East Neuk itself, and to where, beyond the "Dane's Dyke" and "Constantine's Cave", the rocks of Fife Ness plunge their ploughshare into the North Sea, and run a white furrow towards the Carr Rock and Beacon. The road and the railway from St. Andrews keep some distance back from the coast, and following them one misses the "Rock and Spindle", Kinkell and the fantastic Buddo crags. Boarhills, the "bieldy dykes" of Pitmilly, and Kingsbarns remind us that we are traversing what was the "Boar's Chase"—the land gifted to the Church by the Pictish kings, when St. Andrews was known to its Celtic occupants as Muckross or "the Boar's Promontory"—and Kilrymont —"the church on the King's hill". Along this way marched Knox's mob to the assault on the Cathedral, and by the same route, ages before, the defeated hosts of the Northmen surged back to their long-ships, what time

"Kenly's green banks were strewn and overcast
    With arms down-scattered by that populace;
Kinkell, Balrymont, and Balmungo's plain,
    Resounded with the flight of horses and of men".

Farther on, the road strikes across country to Crail, leaving in the plain between it and the sea Cambo, Randerston, Wormiston, Balcomie—homes of the Fife adventurers who went out in King Jamie's time on the vain quest of conquering the Lews from the Macleods—each of them with a nest of legends clinging to its Castle ruin or site.

Crail, the easternmost and one of the quaintest and cleanest of the fishing towns and royal burghs, half converted into watering-places, that fringe the southern hem of Fife, has features it shares with none of its neighbours. It may no longer vend the "speldrins and the Crail capons"—cured salt herrings—for which it was famous, but it takes pride in its wide and umbrageous main street; in the "Batavian graces" of its antique Town Hall; in the site of its royal castle and fortress, girt about by trees shorn by the scythe of the east wind; in the little harbour where the fishing-craft lie snug and safe within the triple arm of protection thrown around them by the rough masonry of the pier, the rocks, and the green braes. Most of all, perhaps, it is proud of the venerable Parish Church of St. Maelrubha, guarding the stone cross, sculptured with strange beasts and half-obliterated devices—possibly the "Auld Rude of Crail" to which pilgrims resorted in pre-Reformation times. From its pulpit Knox, Melville, and Sharp preached various doctrines in various moods: from its high steeple the burghers watched the fight in which Sir Andrew Wood defeated the fleet of the English pirates, and gazed with apprehension as Paul Jones's ships bore up the Firth for Kirkcaldy and Leith. Around it is one of the most interesting country churchyards in Scotland, crowded to overflowing with the symbolism and inscriptions of earlier centuries; and beside its gate is the "Blue Stone of Crail", which fell short when the Devil flung it in a rage from the May Island.

Farther along the shore, past the "Hermit's Well" and the Coves of Caiplie, wherein Adrian and his company, and later, Peden the Prophet, sought shelter from their enemies, and greeted the sun rising behind the May, comes the long and almost continuous line of fisher havens and royal burghs, beginning with Lower Kilrenny, or Cellardyke, and ending with Pittenweem, only to begin again, after a brief interval, with St. Monans, Elie, and Earlsferry. Or if the road instead of the coast be taken, leaving on the right the House of Barns, to which Drummond of Hawthornden came to court the bride he never brought home, one passes through the hamlet of Upper Kilrenny "that became a royal burgh by mistake, and then annexed Cellardyke to ballast it with population". It believes that it

possesses, besides the "Skaith Stane", the grave of
Cardinal Beaton, who was wont to disembark at the
"Cardinal's Steps" at the eastern end of Cellardyke
harbour, or Skinfast-haven—a full-flavoured spot when
the herring-fishing is in full swing.

Each of these little fisher ports has its feet and its
thoughts half immersed in brine; and round its quays
are congregated lofty buildings, often with red-tiled
roofs and weather-beaten fronts or crow-stepped gables
facing the harbour, or newer buildings, that speak of
the ebb and flow of prosperity in gathering the harvest
of the sea.   The rest of its mind is set on attracting the
summer visitor and golfer, or on the business of the
burgh and parish.   Nor, for instance, does Easter and
Wester Anstruther—separated only by the Dreel burn—
forget the store of auld farrant memories these twin
towns have gathered, in the course of the centuries of
their existence, around Town House and market-place,
and Kirk and Kirkyard.   They were curing and ex-
porting fish when Glasgow and Liverpool were places
of little account; and they have sent into the world men
—Thomas Chalmers, for example—who have helped to
turn the current of history in Church and State.   Every-
body, in Fife at least, knows how Rab the Ranter came
to Anster Fair, and played the tune on his pipes to
which Maggie Lauder danced so featly on the East
Green.   But the story is not so familiar of the landing

PITTENWEEM

(Page 49)

here, as related by the inimitable pen of James Melville, minister of Easter Anster—just then setting about the work of building the manse which is still an ornament of the place—of Juan Gomez de Medina, second in command of Philip II's Armada, with thirteen score of survivors from the shipwreck of his hulk on the Fair Isle, "for the maist part young, beardless men, silly, trauchled, and hungered", and of how the citizens of Anster regaled these storm-tossed mariners with "kail, porridge, and fish".

To Pittenweem is but a "spang"; and Pittenweem also has its hoard of ancient houses and traditions, and of lively present-day interests, to give it—what few Fife places lack—a good conceit of itself. Its "weem" or cave can still be discovered, half-way between the beach and the remains of its Augustinian Priory. It is two-chambered, and contains a well, from which may-hap the sainted Fillan has drunk: and a subterranean passage leads, or led, from it to what was the great dining-hall of the Abbey on the terrace above. Little trace is left of this or other mediæval features of Pittenweem; but the tower of the Parish Church, which has arisen on the site, is not unworthy of its position. Pittenweem has always been a "fechtin'" place, and, not content with waging its quarrels at home, has carried them elsewhere. The germ of the "Porteous Riots" was in a tussle between the smugglers and gaugers in what was then a haunt of "free traders".

It was hot even beyond its neighbours in the cause
of the Covenant, and when Charles II, a "Covenanted
Prince", came to this part of Fife in February, 1652, the
town colours were hoisted on the steeple bartizan; the
Bailies and Council met him at the West Port "in their
best apparel", and entertained him at "Robert Smith's
Yett", where a table, "covered with my Lord's best
carpet", was spread with, among other good things,
"great bunnes and other wheat-bread of the best order,
baken with sugar, cannell, and other spices fitting",
and "eight or ten gallons of good strong ale, with
Canary, sack, Rhenish, tent, white and claret wines",
of all which the "Merrie Monarch", after the sound of
"thirty-six cannon shot at once" had died away, no
doubt partook heartily.

Across the golf-links is St. Monans. It, too, has its
holy cave and well; its picturesque groups of old houses
huddled on the shore and along the beach; its restless
sea flashing on reef and harbour wall; and its ancient
and fish-like smells. Above all, it has its Church, much
beloved and often painted by artists, the stumpy tower
and spire rising above the den of the burn and the
fisher houses that cling to its edge and sides like
limpets. It is an interesting specimen of fourteenth-
century Gothic, raised in fulfilment of a vow by King
David Bruce, to celebrate his salvation, through favour
of St. Monan, from being wrecked on the neighbouring

Vows Rocks; and, after itself escaping many dangers of destruction, it is now assured of preservation as a place both of worship and of pilgrimage.

The shell of Newark Castle, built by that David Leslie, Lord Newark, who outmanœuvred Cromwell on the other side of the Firth, until he delivered himself into the Protector's hands at Dunbar; the traces of Ardross Castle, the home of the Dischingtons; and the Lady's Tower, stand between St. Monans and Elie Ness. Here, where Fife bulges out towards the opposite shore, the rocky coast is scalloped like a clam-shell by bay and headland; and on two of the curves are set the sister burghs—one must not say the twin burghs, for the second of the pair boasts of being much the elder—of Elie and Earlsferry. The golf-course is one of their many bonds of union; and each is plentifully endowed with bathing-ground and bracing breezes, and spacious outlooks over firth and fell. There have been many comings and goings at Elie Ness and Chapel Ness since the time of Macduff—his cave is a mile or two farther on near Kincraig Point—or since Brigadier Mackintosh of Borlum crossed over to Lothian with his Highlanders in the '15, to attack Leith and invade England. But it is in comparatively recent years that Earlsferry and Elie have broken from the rough old chrysalis of a trading and fishing town, and have become, in the summer season, butterflies of fashion.

THE FORTH COAST

Round the corner of Kincraig and Ruddons Ness is the great curve of Largo Bay, sweeping away to the west and south-west, where the smoke of collieries and coaling-steamers marks the sites of Methil and Buckhaven, Wemyss and Dysart. In the background are Kilconquhar and its Loch, the woods of Balcarres and Pitcorthie, and the cloven crest of Largo Law. In the foreground, sand and bent for a time take the place of cliff and skerry; and grimy mining and manufacturing industries begin to oust sea-fishing and sea-bathing and golf from ground where they had established prescriptive rights—but not until Largo and its Links are past.

Name and place savour of the salt water. Fisherfolk still "cast their lines in Largo Bay", and bait them on the pier of Lower Largo. Beside it are the birth-place and the monument of Alexander Selkirk or Selcraig, the prototype of that immortal castaway seaman, the "Robinson Crusoe" of Defoe, who was a visitor to the coasts of Fife. Selcraig was

"Nae religious youth,
For at the priest he thrawed his mouth";

and to escape being called to account for unseemly behaviour in church, he ran away to sea. He knew something of buccaneering on the Spanish Main before he was marooned, for four or five years, on Juan Fernandez Island in the Pacific; and he returned to his native village with prize-money and with his Bible, musket, and sea-chest, all of which are extant.

In Upper Largo lived, for half a century after he had left the sea and the Court of James III whom he served so faithfully, another notable sailor, Sir Andrew Wood. It is said that the old Admiral dug a canal, of which some traces are left, so that he might be rowed every Sunday, by a crew of ancient mariners, from Largo House to Largo Church. Behind the Kirk and Kirkton is Kiel's Glen, where, beside the shattered form of Pitcruvie Castle, or on the slopes of the Law, witches used to collogue, when storms were brewing on the Forth, or other mischief was afoot. Witches were almost as plentiful at Largo as at Pittenweem; and the three tall pillars—the "Standing Stones of Lundin", beside the tower and looking down on the Links of the same name—might be the "Weird Sisters" turned to stone while engaged in their unholy rites.

The Links bear also the names of Largo, and Scoonie, and Leven, and are the common property of the villages and holiday-resorts gathered about them, and the delight and solace of thousands of natives and visitors.

After St. Andrews, nothing in Fife can compare in age and fame and spaciousness with the rolling expanse of thymey turf, screened from the sands and the sea by a range of bent-grown hillocks, that extends from the houses of Largo to the Scoonie burn. Leven is big enough to have interests apart from the letting of summer quarters; and between it and Innerleven, once Dubbieside, there falls into the Forth the stream that drains Lochleven, and flows past Leslie and Markinch, Balbirnie, Balgonie, Balfour, and last, but not least, Cameron Bridge, which has produced, along with a famous whisky, Earl Haig. Except the Eden, it is the only Fife stream that can pretend to be a river.

Across the Water of Leven, we are in a Debatable Land where human industry is engaged in persistent struggle with refractory Nature. Methil, not so long since a decayed village and half-deserted haven, has become one of the populous places of Fife, and chief port of shipment of its rich coal-field. It has annexed Innerleven and Buckhaven. It has heaped its coal-bings on the old links of Dubbieside, and cut up inland fields and farms with railway sidings, or covered them with brick-and-mortar. Its docks are canopied with the smoke and steam of locomotives and marine engines, and clamorous with the thunder of the coal discharged from the forest of cranes into the holds of waiting vessels. Buckhaven, once the scaliest and most full-flavoured of fisher towns, pursues its calling among many distractions. An air of neglect and desolation begins to hang over its huddle of tiled roofs, crow-stepped gable-ends and storm-washed "fore-doors", cloven by steep lanes and stairways — even over the "Hyne" itself. The industrial hosts are advancing menacingly towards the ground where Macduff's two-towered Castle and the village of East Wemyss maintain around them a narrowing plot of seclusion and romance.

The shore path threads its way past grottoes opening into the red sandstone rock and along grassy ledges with the waves breaking below on yellow sand, shingly beach, or serried reef. Golf has been abandoned on the old and adventurous Wemyss links, where one had to drive the ball over or across the front of beetling crags, and hole out in the yawning entrance of the Glass Cave, whose roof has recently succumbed to the influence of underground workings. Wemyss Castle still stands high and aloof, fronting the Firth from a rock which is hollowed out into vaulted passages and secret oubliettes, like a "Castle of Otranto". It is surrounded by woods and lawns and gardens that witnessed the brief love-idyll of Mary and Darnley, and guards the heirlooms—including the silver basin given in 1290 by King Eric of Norway to Sir Michael de Wemyss—of possessors who claim descent from the Celtic kings and thanes of Fife.

The humour and the poetry of mining and seafaring life have not been wholly expelled from the village of West Wemyss—the "Barncraig" of Gabriel Setoun. Beyond it, rounding the corners of harbour gables, climbing the waste-heaps and treading warily along the trolley-lines of the pits that, along this piece of coast, extend far under the sea, skirting old castle, chapel, and dovecot walls, and weathering Blair Point, where a "Prisoner of Chillon", sculptured by a pitman's hand, mounts guard over a delightful path slipped in between the rocks and the shore, we come to Dysart.

St. Serf, its patron saint, who chose his anchorite's cell in a cave near the cliff-surrounded harbour and the fine old tower of the former Parish Church that bears his name, would not recognise in the Dysart of to-day the spot where, in the eighth century, he held hot disputation with Satan. Nor, if they were to return, would many of its modern features be identified by "the broad-beamed dealers from Amsterdam and Popperling", who, when the place was known as "Little Holland", came hither to bargain with the "canty carles of Dysart", who exchanged coal and salt, barrels of beer and cured fish, for their "cart wheels and delf-ware, kegs of Hollands and pipes of Rhenish". The stolid front of the Town Hall, and a few corners, moulded doorways, and projecting gables might look familiar. But they would miss the piazzaed fronts, and find that since

ST. MONANS

(Page 50)

their day there had been a slump in witches and
smuggling. Dysart's interests are largely centred in
coal; and while it may find sport and recreation in the
grounds of Dysart House, the Crown domain granted
to the "lordly line of high St. Clair" of Rosslyn, in
recompense for the surrender of the Princedom of
Orkney, it scarcely spares a thought to fling in the
direction of Ravenscraig — fair Rosabelle's shattered
towers, set among rocks and trees overhanging the sea—
that crowns the eastern promontory of Kirkcaldy Bay.

"Kirkcaldy the sell o't", quoth Andrew Fairservice,
"is as lang as any toun in England". For a couple of
miles the streets of the "Lang Toun" are lined along
the sandy shore from the brae and tower of Pathhead
to Linksfield, and another mile or two is strung away
inland by Sinclairtown and Galatown. But long as is
its history as well as its dimensions—for was it not
a thousand years ago the "Church of the Culdees", of
whom the steeple of St. Patrick may be a relic; was it
not famed in later Church annals for the number and
sound doctrine and racy preachings of its dissenting
sects; was not Adam Smith among its natives, and
were not Thomas Carlyle and Edward Irving among its
dominies; was it not the first place in Scotland to
introduce power-loom weaving, and is it not pervaded
to this hour by the smell of its thriving floorcloth and
linoleum industries?—Kirkcaldy must not detain us.

Across the Tiel, flowing under Balwearie Castle, and Seafield, the empty shell of a peel tower marks the sea boundary of the lands of Grange, the heritage of Sir William Kirkaldy, the champion of Mary Stuart; and a mile or two more of rocky coast brings us to Kinghorn. Here, too, there is plenty of material to engage the mind and the eye—in the ancient houses of the Overgait, the Nethergait, and the Cunzie Neuk; in the church and churchyard on the shore, with the old mansion behind that lodged Archbishop Sharp on his last crossing to Fife; in streets that remind us by their names that Bruces and Balliols and other kingly personages made Kinghorn their halting-place or residence; and in the links and old harbour of Petticur, under the headland that guards, along with Inchkeith, the northern passage of the Forth.

A mile nearer Burntisland, a basaltic crag overhangs the road and the Long Sands, and under it is the monument that points to the traditional spot where Alexander III met with his death, while riding to his castle on Kinghorn Ness. Burntisland, once known as Wester Kinghorn, has supplanted the older and more easterly burgh as the ferry-town to Lothian. It sets more store by its coal-shipping trade, and its accommodation for summer visitors on the margin of its links or under the steep declivities of its Bin hill. It is not behind its neighbours, however, in antique dwellings, hidden, for the most part, in back streets adjoining the big square parish church, built after a sixteenth-century Amsterdam model, that dominates the harbour and the railway station. Burntisland has yet older ties with the past, in the ruined Church of St. Adamnan in the Kirkton, and in the peninsulated Rossend Castle, now a boarding-house, with panelled rooms and hiding-places in the thickness of the walls, where Abbot Durie of Dunfermline concealed the relics of Saint Margaret until the Reformation storm blew over, and Chastelard lay perdu when he made his mad and fatal attempt to invade the privacy of Mary, Queen of Scots.

The Hawes Wood, between Burntisland and Aberdour, is not the enchanting walk it was before the railway was drawn across it. But it is still a pleasant path, in fine weather, for the holiday visitors who throng these shores. At the western end it debouches on White Sands Bay and on the Hawk Craig and Aberdour.

In summer weather migrant flocks of seekers of rest and pleasure flit to these grateful shades and sunny outlooks. They crowd the upper and lower villages, fast losing all trace of the time when Aberdour was the abode of hand-loom weaving; they overflow the beaches, where the groups of picnickers, bathers, and loungers are diversified by an occasional ice-cream merchant or pierrot troupe, and lively love - making takes place under the trees or beside the boulders on the shore; they flock to the headland that looks down upon the steamer's landing-stage and the little harbour —dry at low water—of this "dimple on the stern lineaments of Fife", and on the yachts and sailing-boats sprinkled over the bay. To the eastward the wooded coast, backed by the Cullalo hills, can be traced to Burntisland; to the west the Ferry Hills and the limbs of the Forth Bridge are in sight. In the near or farther distance islands are spread on the waters of the Firth—Inchkeith, Cramond, Mickery and Mickery Stone, Craigdimas and the Haystack, but more in evidence, Inchcolm, only a mile or two away. Naval buildings, reared beside the site of the hermitage and cell where Alexander the Fiery found shelter with the anchorite, are now more prominent than the tower of the twelfth-century abbey church. Opposite are the sylvan shores of Dalmeny, while Edinburgh Castle, Arthur's Seat, and the Pentlands—the vision that, in clear weather, everywhere accompanies those who follow these coasts of Fife—are outlined on the southern horizon.

At the head of the bight, where the Dour comes down to the sea, are the grounds of Aberdour House, the home of Earl Beatty's family in war-time, and beside it the old Castle of the Douglases, its burly dovecot, and the bell-tower and ivied gable of the roofless

BUCKHAVEN

(Page 55)

Church of St. Fillan. The Castle, still a possession
of the House of Morton, is also a ruin, only two or
three rooms in the newer part, raised before the fortunes of the builder began to crumble with those of
Charles I, being habitable; and one may ask in vain
for the whereabouts of the Holy Well, the earlier lure
that brought hosts of pilgrims to Aberdour.

Round the Bell Point, whence the monks of Inchcolm embarked for their island across Mortimer's
Deep, is Dalgety Bay. At the head of it is another
deserted and ruined pre-Reformation church, in which
is buried that Chancellor Seton who built Fyvie Castle
and Pinkie House, and was a mighty man in the
counsels of James VI; while farther on are the bare
walls of Donibristle. The wing of the house from
which the "Bonnie Earl" fled out of the fire into the
darkness and the shelter of the neighbouring shore
rocks from his slayers, is intact, and preserves relics
of this and of other passages in the history of the
family of the Stuarts, Earls of Moray, descendants of
the "Good Regent", who continue to be the lords
of this stately domain.

The little coaling-port of St. David's and a strip
of bare shore separate Donibristle from Inverkeithing,
once, as has been seen, one of the royal residences
in Fife, and a seaport that competed with Leith in
trade and importance. Its shallow, circular tidal basin,

which could accommodate the war and merchant ships
of the early Stuarts, can now afford shelter only to
the trawlers attached to the Fleet. Its Carmelite
monastery, where the last Culdee Assembly was held,
has disappeared; the tower of St. Peter's, and the
fine armorial font, are all that is left of the pre-Reformation Parish Church, founded in 1120. Rothwells
Inn, Queen Annabella's "palace", with the attached
"Chapel Royal", has been used as a lodging-house for
the navvies employed at the Forth Bridge and Rosyth
works.

The Ferry Hills reach out into the Firth, diminish-
ing, by more than half, the distance between the opposing shores. On their crown is a golf-course, and
through the limestone rock bores the railway to the
Bridge, which, in two spans of a third of a mile each,
making use of Inchgarvie as a stepping-stone, clears
the intervening space by a steel structure that rises
370 feet above high water, and leaves a height of
150 feet under each arch for vessels entering or leaving
St. Margaret's Hope. From time immemorial, and
especially since Queen Margaret found shelter in it,
this "Portus Reginæ" has been found the shortest
and safest means of access to Fife. And here has
been realized, with a difference, the dream of the
thirteenth century Jew who tried to found, on the
Carlingnose promontory, out of which the stones of

many London streets have been quarried, a "New Jerusalem", where would be gathered all the trade of the coast, and "a harbour of refuge would be established for a distressed nation". The warships of the Empire—the leviathans and the shrimps of the Royal Navy—now ride in these smoother waters, between shores less chafed by the waves, waiting their turn for duty on the high seas, or for taking on board supplies or refitting in the docks of Rosyth. On one side are the burgh of South Queensferry, the Palladian front and terraced woods of Hopetoun, and the headlands on which are set Blackness Castle and the town of Bo'ness. From the northern shore there project into the Upper Firth quay-walls, loading-berths, and graving-docks, surmounted by a forest of huge cranes and derricks, while other buildings and appurtenances of a Naval Base occupy the shore, beset the Castle and Doocot, and old Kirk and Kirkyard—the only memorials left to Rosyth of its past—and stretch across the intervening hills towards the spires and towers of Royal Dunfermline.

That seat of kings is only as yet a background to the Shores of Fife, and its place in history has already been sketched. To-day it discovers more practical interest in developing housing schemes and improving communications in the direction of the Base, and in the manifold intellectual and material activities of the Trust founded by its generous son, the late Andrew Carnegie, than in the story of Malcolm and Margaret, of Bruce and the Jameses, and in the ancient glories of Abbey and Palace. Yet here, as inextricably as anywhere on the fringes of the " Kingdom ", the strands of the past and present are interwoven. The square keep of Rosyth Castle rises, surrounded on three sides by the sea, near the spot where Margaret landed. It became the property of her descendants, the Stuarts of Rosyth and Durrisdeer. Mary Stuart lived in it; at least her initials and arms, with the date 1561, are carved over the main entrance. It is strange how constantly, on the Shores of Fife, the threads in the strongly contrasted lives and destinies of these royal ladies, Margaret and Mary, are brought together! And although it is a delusion, shared by Queen Victoria, that Oliver Cromwell's mother, who was a Stuart, was born at Rosyth, it is possible that the Protector occupied the Castle when he was vouchsafed the "unspeakable mercy" of his victory on the adjoining fields.

Mary is said to have embarked at Limekilns after her flight from Lochleven. The village and haven, and "King's Cellar", crouching under the Gellet Crag and the woods of Lord Elgin's seat of Broomhall, will be interesting in many eyes as the place from which David Balfour and Alan Breck Stewart escaped in a boat to Queensferry and the Hawes Inn. A little to the west is

DYSART

(Page 56)

the coaling-port of Charlestown, and Ironmill Bay and Crombie interpose between Charlestown and what we may call the last lap of Fife. Here, also, military and naval works have invaded a once almost deserted shore, have encamped around the ferry-haven at Crombie Point, extended its pier a stage nearer Bo'ness opposite, and beset the lonely yew-fringed graveyard and church walls overlooking the Firth. On the margin of Culross Bay the view to the west opens up into the heart of the Highlands; the waters narrow away to a point, and the Forth becomes a river. At low water the tidal flats reach out to the spectral shape of the ruined salt-pans on Preston Island; and the foreshore is covered with a dingy mud, the exuvium deposited by the reclamation of Flanders Moss in the eighteenth century. It was in cleaner water, one may hope, that the poor old women of Torryburn were drowned at the stake off the green ness of that village by the witch-finding zeal of the Rev. Allan Logan, the Fife Cotton Mather.

Torryburn, Newmill, and Low Valleyfield form a practically unbroken line of houses, drawn up along the shore, in single or double file, to the border of their "auld enemy", Culross. The railway carried along the beach, and the coal-pit opened on the shore, have restored the prosperity of these venerable villages, but have sadly spoiled their charm. Behind them, on sharply rising ground, are the trees of Craigflower, Torry, Valleyfield, and Culross Abbey; and there is a higher drive along this winding coast, the views from which have been boldly compared to those from the Cornice Roads of the Riviera. There are many things to be noted on the way — among them Duni-quarle; the Bluther burn that formerly divided Fife from Perth; the old Bede-houses; the "Backet Pat", where Scott's friend, Sir Robert Preston, the founder of the Greenwich Whitebait Dinners, kept his turtles; and the birth-place of St. Mungo. And here already we are on the "Cooross causeys".

In spite of the intrusion of latter-day contraptions, the ancient burgh remains a genuine relic and museum of the past. The cobbled ways that come plunging down between high walls, from the level of the Abbey Church to the shore; the group of ancient houses, corbelled, turreted, and crow-stepped, with devices and dates going back to the sixteenth century, that gather about the Cross, and the Sandgait, and the Playfield; the "hanging gardens" behind them that climb the steep bank and seem to prop up the woods of Balgowan and keep them from tumbling down into the streets, remind us of the prosperous times when Culross enter-tained kings and princes, and housed families of noble birth, Bruces and Erskines, Cochranes and Primroses, who did not disdain to share in the profits of its coal and salt trade, and when its "girdles" (griddles) were renowned throughout the "Land of Cakes".

Up at the Abbey, one is on still deeper historic mould. It is the spot where Servanus served and taught, and Kentigern, or Mungo, worked the miracles symbolized on the arms of his city of Glasgow. Of the Cistercian House, founded in 1217 by Malcolm, Earl of Fife, some considerable fragments of the cloister and refectory remain to tell of its former extent and magnificence, and a portion of the chapter-house has recently been uncovered. The nave, which became the church of the burgh after the abandonment of a still older edifice, of which the walls are standing, has almost disappeared. It was separated by the massive tower from the choir, the church of the monks, now restored and become a goodly and deeply impressive place of prayer. It seems to focus within its walls the family and burghal memories, along with the art relics and ecclesiastical traditions of the district — from the stone coffin of the founder's date to monuments and armorial blazonry of the races that in later times have owned lands and exercised influence in this part of Western Fife—among them Blackadders; Campbells of Argyll, whose "Castle Gloom" is at the foot of the Ochils, not far away; Cochranes of Dundonald, inventors and sea-heroes; Prestons of Valleyfield; and Bruces of Carnock, one of whom, Edward, Lord Kinloss, killed in a duel in the Low Countries in 1613, bequeathed his heart to Culross Abbey.

Culross, it has been said, is "hard to get at, but still harder to get away from". Beyond it, to the west, are the imposing, if somewhat funereal, aspects of Dunimarle, with the battlefield on the heights behind— the last on our list of "Macduff" sites; and the woods of Sands interpose before Kincardine-on-Forth and Tulliallan Castle, and the limits of the County of Fife are reached.

At the ferry of the old barony burgh of Kincardine, which was at one time noted for its salt-pans and shipbuilding and whaling industries, and for its whisky, the Firth has already become a river, which winds in wide curves through the fat carse lands, on which at full tide the embanked waters appear to look down. The opposing banks have approached to hailing distance; the Ochils and Stirling Castle and the Abbey Craig, crowned by Wallace's Monument, have drawn near; there is an end to the Shores of Fife.

Printed and bound in Great Britain